Securing a Level 3 Mathematics

Hilary Koll and Steve Mills

Contents

RISING STARS

Rising Stars UK Ltd.
7 Hatchers Mews, Bermondsey Street, London SE1 3GS
www.risingstars-uk.com

Every effort has been made to trace copyright holders and obtain their permission for the use of copyright materials. The authors and publisher will gladly receive information enabling them to rectify any error or omission in subsequent editions.

All facts are correct at time of going to press.

Published 2010
Reprinted 2011

Authors: Hilary Koll and Steve Mills
Consultant Maths Publisher: Jean Carnall
Text design: Laura de Grasse
Typesetting: Ray Rich
Artwork: David Woodroffe
Cover Design: Burville-Riley Partnership

British Library Cataloguing in Publication Data.
A CIP record for this book is available from the British Library.

ISBN: 978-1-84680-717-6

Printed by Craft Print International Limited, Singapore.

Using Shine!

This book will help you secure a level 3 in maths and focuses on key areas that pupils working at level 2 and level 3 often find difficult. Getting to grips with these areas will help you to move up a level.

1. Take a **System scan** to check out areas you need to work on.

2. **Go to page** ...   Go to page   to find questions, games and activities to help.

3. **Plug in** to the topic with a quick warm up.

4. Use the **Chat room** to discuss mathematics with a partner.

5. **Power up** and work on the trickier parts of the topic.

6. Try a game in **Game play** for more practice.

7. Use the **Explore** activity to apply your knowledge.

Look at out for the photocopy masters for extra help,

or for a larger version of a game.

Unit 1 – System scan A

1 What is the value of each red digit in these numbers?

a 63   b 37   c 408

d 786   e 924   f 300

2 Using digits, write the number that is one more than each of these.

a ninety-nine   b two hundred and twelve

c three hundred and twenty-six   d eight hundred and three

e five hundred and ninety-nine   f six hundred and nine

Go to page 12

3 Write the largest number in each set.

a 463, 364, 634   b 209, 902, 920

c 747, 474, 477   d 303, 330, 333, 296

e 400, 487, 440, 407   f 504, 455, 505, 499

4 Multiply each number by 10.

a 6   b 9   c 46   d 39   e 60

5 Divide each number by 10.

a 80   b 20   c 880   d 520   e 400

Go to page 14

6 Round these numbers.

a Round 72 to the nearest 10.   b Round 529 to the nearest 100.

c Round 168 to the nearest 10.   d Round 487 to the nearest 100.

e Round 435 to the nearest 10.   f Round 250 to the nearest 100.

Go to page 16

7 Write the value of each number marked on this line.

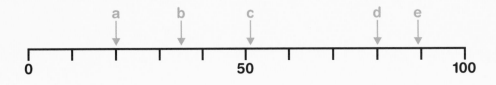

Unit 1 – System scan B

1 Which number in each set is the smallest?

   a –6, 0, 4   b 5, –2, –6   c –8, –5, 1

   d –4, –3, –5   e 7, –1, –7   f 2, –2, –1

Go to page 18

2 Write the price of each toy in pounds.

60p   **75p**   **120p**

3 How many 10p coins are needed to make £1.50?

Go to page 20

4 A table is 1.35 m long.
How long is it in centimetres?

5 A pencil is three-tenths of a metre long. Write its length in metres.

6 What fraction of each pattern is red?

a    b 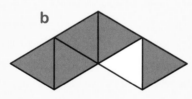   c

Go to page 22

d

7 Write each of these lengths as a fraction of a metre.

   a 7 cm   b 43 cm   c 89 cm

1 Use the fact in the blue box to help you answer each of these questions.

$5 + 8 = 13$

Go to page 24

- a $13 - 8 =$
- b $5 + 9 =$
- c $50 + 80 =$
- d $130 - 80 =$
- e $85 + 8 =$
- f $5 + 68 =$
- g $73 - 8 =$
- h $230 - 50 =$

2 Write two addition facts and two subtraction facts for each of the blue boxes.

- a $7 + 8 = 15$ _____ _____ _____ _____
- b $13 - 6 = 7$ _____ _____ _____ _____

Go to page 26

3 Write a number sentence for each of these problems and find the answer.

- a A piece of strawberry lace is 100 cm long. I cut some off. It is now 22 cm long. How much did I cut off?

- b Some people are in a shop. 85 more arrive, making 100 people in total. How many were there at first?

- c James is given some money. He spends £38 of it. He now has £48. How much was he given?

Go to page 28

4 Work these out in your head.

- a $3\ 8 + 5\ 7 =$
- b $4\ 2 + 2\ 9 =$
- c $7\ 1 - 3\ 4 =$
- d $9\ 3 - 3\ 9 =$

Go to page 30

Unit 3 – System scan

1 Write one addition and two multiplication facts to show the number of spots in each set.

a

b

Go to page 32

2 Answer these division questions.

a 16 ÷ 4 =

b 20 ÷ 2 =

c 18 ÷ 3 =

d 24 ÷ 3 =

e 20 ÷ 5 =

f 21 ÷ 3 =

Go to page 34

3 Write two multiplication facts for each group.

a

b

c △ △ △ △ △ △
△ △ △ △ △ △
△ △ △ △ △ △
△ △ △ △ △

Go to page 36

4 Use this diagram to help you work out 4 × 26.

| 20 | 6 |

4 | 4 × 20 | 4 × 6 |

5 Find:

a 83 ÷ 5 =

b 67 ÷ 4 =

c 52 ÷ 3 =

Go to page 38

6 Find the fraction of each amount of money.

a $\frac{1}{4}$ of £12

b $\frac{1}{5}$ of £20

c $\frac{5}{6}$ of £60

d $\frac{2}{3}$ of £15

e $\frac{7}{8}$ of £24

f $\frac{3}{4}$ of £32

Go to page 40

Unit 4 – System scan

1 Write whether each statement is **true** or **false**.

a This is a
pentagon.

b This is a
regular shape.

c This is a
hexagon.

Go to page 42

or any page in Unit 4

2 Which of these shapes has
been put in the wrong place?

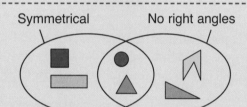

---

3 Write whether each statement is **true** or **false**.

a This is a cone.

b This is a cylinder.

c This is a prism.

Go to page 44

or any page in Unit 4

4 Which of these shapes has
been put in the wrong place?

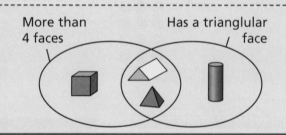

---

5 Jo has a solid shape with 6 identical square faces. What is the shape called?

6 Li has drawn a flat shape with 5 sides and 5 corners. What is it called?

Go to page 46

or any page in Unit 4

7 Kim is holding a shape with 2 circular faces and 1 curved face.
What is it called?

---

8 Which is the next shape in the sequence?

A   B   C

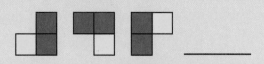 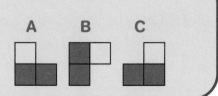

Go to page 46

or any page in Unit 4

1 Look at the ice skating sign.

£5 per adult
£3 per child
and £2 skate hire

Go to page 50

How much does it cost, including skate hire, for:

a 2 adults and 3 children?

b 4 adults and 2 children?

2 a Two identical parcels together weigh 1 kg. A smaller parcel weighs 10 g less than one of them. What is its mass?

b Two identical parcels each weigh 400 g. A larger parcel weighs $\frac{1}{2}$ kg more than one of them. What is the total mass of the parcels?

Go to page 52

3 How long is each film?

a **SPACE APE**
Starts at 6:15
Finishes at 9:45

b **Bond Again**
Starts at 6:45
Finishes at 9:30

4 What time does each film start?

a **INVADERS!**
Lasts $2\frac{1}{2}$ hours
Finishes at 8:15

b **Ice Attack!**
Lasts $3\frac{3}{4}$ hours
Finishes at 5:30

Go to page 54

5 Answer these word problems.

a A TV show starts at 4:30. It lasts for $1\frac{3}{4}$ hours. At what time does it end?

b Three-quarters of an hour ago, a TV show started at 5:35. What time is it now?

c A quarter of an hour ago, a TV show started at five to six. What time is it now?

1 Look at this pictogram.

Blackbird	
Robin	
Sparrow	
Magpie	
Greenfinch	

 = 2 birds

a How many robins were at the bird table?

b How many sparrows were at the bird table?

c How many more greenfinches than magpies were seen?

d How many birds were seen altogether?

Go to page 56

or any other page in Unit 6

2 Look at this table.

	Week 1	Week 2	Week 3
Art club	11	15	16
Netball club	16	16	14
Football club	11	12	12

a How many children went to netball club in week 3?

b How many children went to football club in week 1?

c How many more children went to art club than football club in week 2?

Go to page 58

or any other page in Unit 6

3 Look at the Carroll diagram.

a Which number is incorrectly placed?

b Where should the number 24 be placed?

	Multiples of 4	Not multiples of 4
Multiples of 5	16, 20	5, 10, 15
Not multiples of 5	4, 8, 12	1, 2, 3, 6, 7, 9, 11, 13, 14, 17, 18, 19

1 What number is each arrow pointing to?

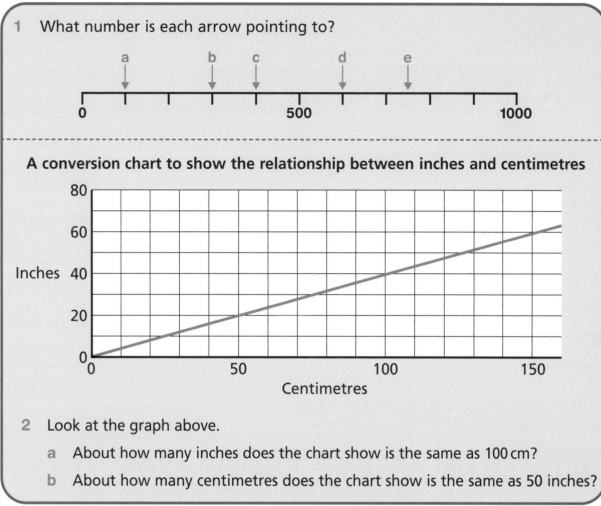

A conversion chart to show the relationship between inches and centimetres

Go to
page 60

or any
other page
in Unit 6

2 Look at the graph above.

a About how many inches does the chart show is the same as 100 cm?

b About how many centimetres does the chart show is the same as 50 inches?

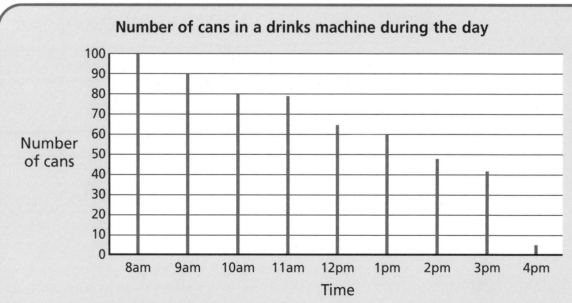

Number of cans in a drinks machine during the day

Go to
page 62

or any
other page
in Unit 6

3 Look at the graph above.

a How many cans were sold between 8am and 9am?

b Between which two hours were the most cans sold?

c About how many cans were sold between 8am and 4pm?

The value of digits

 Plug in

1 Count on in 1s from 95 to 105.

95   96   97

2 Count on in 10s from 170 to 270.

170 180 190

3 Count on in 10s from 445.

445 455 465

4 Count on in 10s from 677.

677 687

5 Count on in 10s from 403.

403

 Power up

James works at a bank.

1 He needs to write the number of pounds on each slip of paper in words.
   Can you help him?

| **£92** | **£810** | **£361** | **£540** | **£205** | **£403** |

2 Each amount of money can be made using £100 notes, £10 notes and £1 coins.

   a Draw a table like this and fill in how many of each note or coin is needed to make each amount.

	£100 notes	£10 notes	£1 coins
£92			
£810			
£361			
£540			
£205			
£403			

   b What do you notice about the digits?

Chat room

Talk to a partner about what this diagram shows.

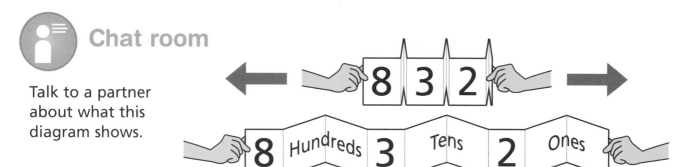

Now, with your partner say what each of these would show when stretched. Then arrange them in order, smallest first.

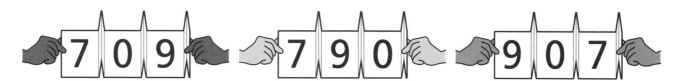

Game play

2+ players

You will need: a set of place value cards from PCM 1 for each player.

- Spread your set of cards face down on the table.
- Each player picks a small, medium and large card from their set and puts them together to make a number.
- The player with the largest number scores a point.

Explore

Copy the grid and letters. Use the clues to put the right number in each box.

E is the number four hundred and seven.

B is fifty more than E.

C is two hundred more than B.

G is seven less than C.

F is ten less than G.

D is 8 more than F.

A is sixty more than D.

H is two more than A.

I is seven hundred less than H.

A	B	C
D	E	F
G	H	I

Multiplying and dividing by 10

 Plug in

Write this sequence in full, filling in the missing numbers.

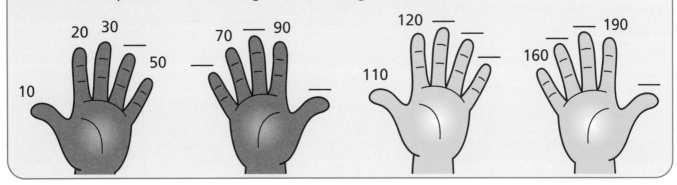

 Chat room (1)

Talk to a partner about what the text in the box is telling you.

Multiplying by 10

When multiplying by 10, move each digit one place to the left.

$29 \times 10 = 290$

	H	T	U
		2	9
	2	9	0

 Power up

1 Jo plants 10 seeds in each pot.

Write how many seeds are in each row of pots.

a

b

c

d

e

f A row with 11 pots.

g A row with 26 pots.

h A row with 52 pots.

2 Multiply each number by 10.

a 7   b 45   c 80   d 71   e 49   f 90

Chat room (2)

Talk to a partner about what the text in the box is telling you.

Dividing by 10

When dividing by 10, move each digit one place to the right.

$290 \div 10 = 29$

H	T	U
2	9	0
	2	9 . 0

29.0 is the same as 29

Together, use what you have learnt to divide each of these numbers by 10.

a 30   b 420   c 800   d 510   e 470   f 500

 Game play

2 players

You will need a counter each and a dice.

- Take turns to roll the dice and move your counter forward and answer the question.
- If both players land on a question with the same answer you must both go back to the start.

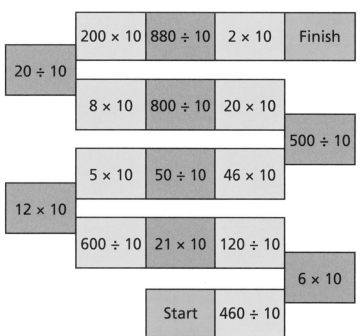

 Explore

We use multiplying by 10 to change centimetres into millimetres. This is because there are 10 millimetres in one centimetre. Use a ruler to measure these lines in centimetres. Then write how many millimetres each line is.

1 _____

2 _____

3 _____

Number lines and rounding

Plug in

Write the number halfway between the two numbers in each pair.

a   0 and 100   b   0 and 20   c   40 and 50   d   50 and 100

e   200 and 300   f   600 and 800   g   0 and 500   h   0 and 1000

Power up

Each station shows a multiple of 10. Each train stops at the station nearest to its number.

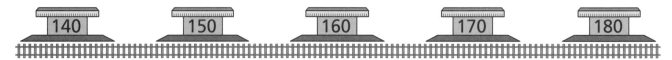

1   Write which station each train will stop at, by rounding to the nearest 10.

a   148   b   167   c   153   d   174   e   157   f   176

2   What if the number was 165?

3   There are stations at every multiple of 10. Round these numbers to the nearest 10 to find where these trains will stop.

a   256   b   382   c   415   d   801   e   297   f   109

4   Each sign along a road shows a multiple of 100.

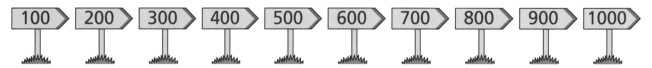

Round each of these numbers to the nearest 100.

a   b   c   d   e   f

744   623   875   450   949   139

Chat room

Talk to a partner and agree together what number you think each arrow is pointing to.

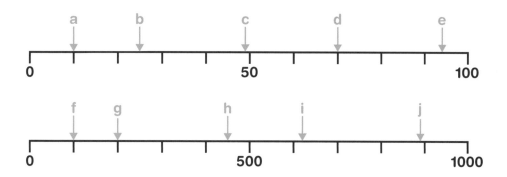

Game play

2 players

You will need: place value cards from PCM 1.

- Each player writes the multiples of 100 from 0 to 1000.

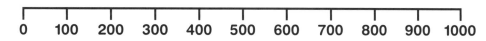

- Spread the cards face down on the table.
- Take turns to pick a small, medium and large card to make a 3-digit number.
- Round the number to the nearest 100 and, if you can, cross off the multiple of 100 from your list.
- The winner is the player to cross off most multiples from their list after ten turns each.

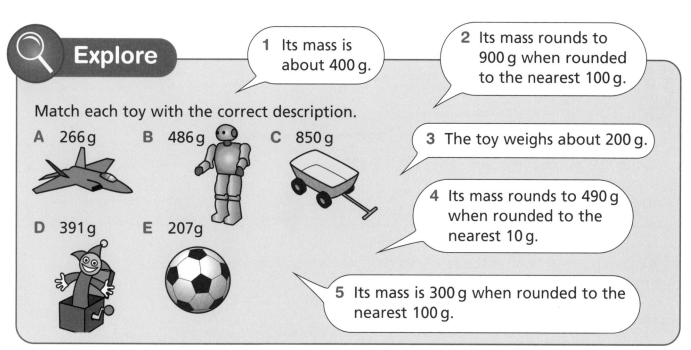

Explore

Match each toy with the correct description.

A 266 g   B 486 g   C 850 g

D 391 g   E 207 g

1 Its mass is about 400 g.

2 Its mass rounds to 900 g when rounded to the nearest 100 g.

3 The toy weighs about 200 g.

4 Its mass rounds to 490 g when rounded to the nearest 10 g.

5 Its mass is 300 g when rounded to the nearest 100 g.

Positive and negative numbers

 Plug in

Write which temperature is colder in each pair, using the thermometer to help you.

a   6°C or –1°C

b   –5°C or 0°C

c   –3°C or 3°C

d   –5°C or –6°C

e   –3°C or –7°C

f   1°C or –8°C

 ## Chat room

Look at the information in the box with a partner.

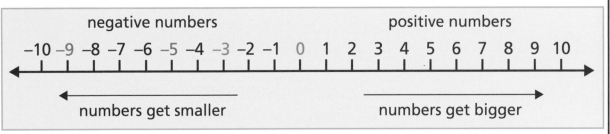

Talk about whether you think each statement below is **true** or **false**.

> When we read the number –3 it is called 'minus three' or 'negative three'.

> The number –9 is larger than the number –5.

> Negative numbers are always less than zero.

> Negative numbers are like a 'reflection' of the numbers on the other side of zero.

 ## Power up

1   Leaves have fallen in the playground and covered some numbers.

Write the number hidden under each leaf.

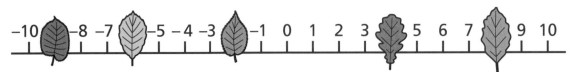

2   Find these numbers on the line and then write them in order of size, starting with the smallest: –2, 8, 3, 0, –10, –6

Game play

2 players

You will need: a 5p coin and two dice.

- Place the 5p on zero.
- One player wins if the coin passes – 10, the other if it passes 10.
- Take turns to roll the dice and find the total.

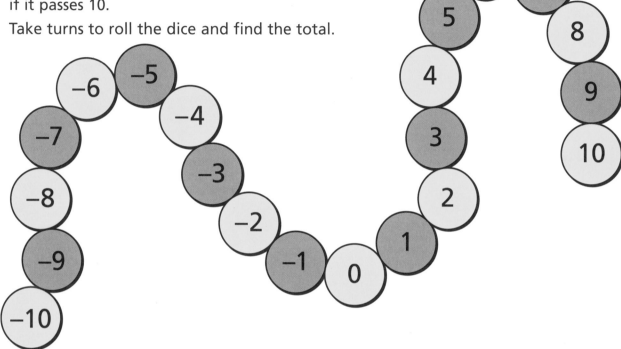

- Move the 5p according to the totals shown below.

Total	2	3	4	5	6	7	8	9	10	11	12
Move	Up 8	Down 7	Down 5	Up 3	Down 2	Down 1	Up 2	Down 3	Up 5	Up 7	Down 8

 ## Explore

Work out the midday temperature each day during one week, using these clues.

- Monday was the warmest when it was 3°C at midday.
- Tuesday was 2 degrees colder than Monday.
- It was 3 degrees colder on Wednesday than on Tuesday.
- On Thursday it was 2 degrees colder than on Wednesday.
- Friday was the coldest day when it was –6°C at midday.
- On Saturday the temperature rose by 3 degrees.
- On Sunday it was 1 degree warmer than on Saturday.

Monday	3°C
Tuesday	°C
Wednesday	°C
Thursday	°C
Friday	°C
Saturday	°C
Sunday	°C

Decimals – money and measures

Copy and complete these sequences.

a   10p 20p 30p ____ ____ ____ ____ ____ ____ 100p

b   £0.10 £0.20 £0.30 ____ ____ ____ ____ ____ ____ £1.00

c   10cm 20cm 30cm ____ ____ ____ ____ ____ ____ 100cm

d   0.1m 0.2m 0.3m ____ ____ ____ ____ ____ ____ 1m

 Chat room

The sequences above are grouped in pairs. Talk to a partner about what you notice about each pair of sequences. These pictures may help you.

 Power up

1   There are two ways of writing amounts of money: in pounds and in pence.
    For each toy, write the price in pounds and in pence.

a
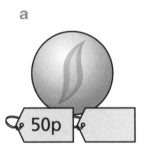
50p

b

40p

c

£0.70

d
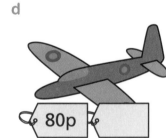
80p

e
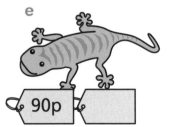
90p

f

£0.85

g
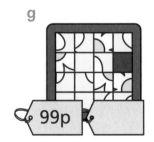
99p

h
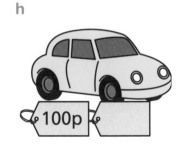
100p

2   These measurements can also be written in two ways. Write them in both ways.

Tip: 0.5 m is the same as 0.50 m. | 50 cm | = | 0.5 m |

a [   ] | 0.7 m | b | 40 cm | [   ]   c [   ] | 0.9 m |

d [   ] | 0.25 m | e | 65 cm | [   ]   f [   ] | 0.72 m |

 Game play

1 player

You will need: coloured cubes/counters in red, blue, green, yellow and white (at least four in each colour).

● Place coloured cubes/counters onto the squares below the line to match those above with the same value.

| two-tenths of a pound | 30p | twenty-three 10p coins | 2.3 m | 30 cm |

| £0.20 | three 10p coins | 230 cm | three strips of 10 cm | twenty-three strips of 10 cm | 20p | 0.3 m |

| £0.30 | three-tenths of a pound | 230p | two 10p coins | three-tenths of a metre | £2.30 |

 Explore

Work with a partner. You will need a metre stick.
Measure the lengths of some items less than a metre around the classroom.

Write each measurement in centimetres, for example 64 cm, and in metres, for example 0.64 m.

Understanding fractions

Plug in

Use the pictures to help you write the fractions in each set in order from smallest to largest.

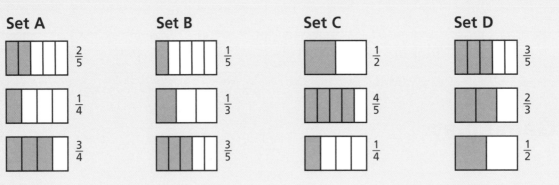

Set A $\frac{2}{5}$ $\frac{1}{4}$ $\frac{3}{4}$

Set B $\frac{1}{5}$ $\frac{1}{3}$ $\frac{3}{5}$

Set C $\frac{1}{2}$ $\frac{4}{5}$ $\frac{1}{4}$

Set D $\frac{3}{5}$ $\frac{2}{3}$ $\frac{1}{2}$

Chat room

Talk to a partner about your answers to the Plug in activity.
What fraction of this chocolate bar is brown?
Who is correct and why?

 $\frac{8}{2}$ is brown.

 $\frac{2}{8}$ is brown.

 $\frac{8}{10}$ is brown.

 $\frac{10}{8}$ is brown.

Power up

What fraction of each rug is coloured? Count the number of equal parts altogether to give the denominator (the bottom number). Then count the coloured parts to give the numerator (the top number).

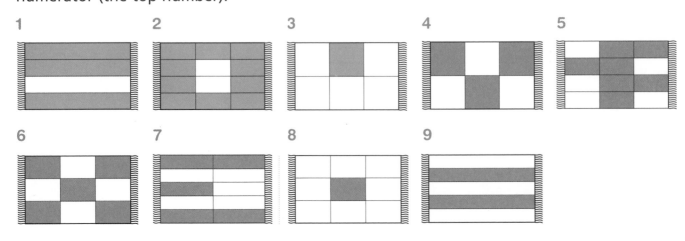

1 2 3 4 5

6 7 8 9

Game play

2 players

Your teacher will give you PCM 2.

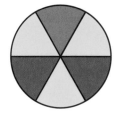

- Colour the kaleidoscope patterns to match the fractions and then cut out the cards to play this game.

- Spread all the cards face down on the table and mix them up.

- Choose a colour and then each turn over a card of that colour.

- The player with the largest fraction wins a point.

- Place the cards face down again and choose a new colour.

- The winner is the first player to reach 6 points.

$\frac{1}{6}$ is red

$\frac{2}{6}$ is blue

$\frac{3}{6}$ is yellow

Explore

Work out the missing fractions.

1 a 1cm is ☐ of a metre.   **b** 3cm is ☐ of a metre.

   c 11cm is ☐ of a metre.   **d** 99cm is ☐ of a metre.

Clue: How many centimetres are in a metre? This is the bottom number (denominator).

2 a 1p is ☐ of a pound.   **b** 17p is ☐ of a pound.

   c 67p is ☐ of a pound.   **d** 99p is ☐ of a pound.

Clue: How many pence are in a pound? This is the bottom number (denominator).

3 a 1g is ☐ of a kilogram.   **b** 57g is ☐ of a kilogram.

   c 388g is ☐ of a kilogram.   **d** 750g is ☐ of a kilogram.

Clue: How many grams are in a kilogram? This is the bottom number (denominator).

Write yourself a note about what you have learnt in this lesson.

Using known facts to find others

Plug in

How quickly can you write the answers to these questions?

a 6 + 4	b 13 – 9	c 6 + 7	d 3 + 8	e 9 – 5	f 7 + 7	g 4 + 7
h 16 – 8	i 7 + 8	j 12 – 8	k 7 + 5	l 9 + 8	m 13 – 8	n 6 + 8

Game play

2 players

You will need: a coin, 8 counters (4 of one colour and 4 of another) and a dice.

- Take turns to roll the dice and move the coin around the trail.
- Answer the question you land on and find the answer in the centre.
- If you find it, cover it with one of your coloured counters if you can.
- The winner is the first to have four counters in a line.

Trail (clockwise from top-left):
140 – 80, 50 + 50, 130 – 40, 70 + 70, 50 + 90, 110 – 20, 140 – 70, 60 + 40, 70 + 50, 70 + 80, 90 + 20, 80 + 80, 70 + 40, 60 + 50, 170 – 90, 70 + 90, 60 + 80, 80 + 50, 130 – 60, 80 + 90, 80 + 30, 60 + 90, 170 – 80, 60 + 30, 130 – 70, 40 + 80, 120 – 70, 90 + 40, 150 – 70, 30 + 80, 60 + 70

Centre grid:
80	170	70	90	60	110	70	80
50	140	160	80	150	140	170	60
110	60	90	150	70	50	90	130
120	110	150	100	120	130	190	90
80	70	180	60	90	80	180	90

Chat room

Tell a partner how you could use the fact in the box to answer each of the questions.

6 + 7 = 13

7 + 6 =

6 + 8 =

13 − 7 =

60 + 70 =

46 + 7 =

63 − 7 =

 Power up

Use the fact in the blue box to help you answer the questions.

7 + 8 = 15

a   15 − 8 =

b   7 + 9 =

c   70 + 80 =

d   150 − 80 =

e   67 + 8 =

f   7 + 28 =

g   75 − 8 =

h   95 − 7 =

Explain to a partner how you worked each question out.

 Explore

Write a number sentence for each of these problems using the fact in the red box to help you.

74 − 28 = 46

1   There are 74 kg of potatoes in a shop and 46 kg are sold. How many kilograms are left?

2   There are 460 children at a football match. 280 more children arrive. How many children are there altogether?

3   There are 28 sheep in a field. 46 more arrive. How many are there now?

4   Jo has £74. He spends £46. How much has he now?

5   Pete has a 740 cm piece of string. He cuts off 280 cm. How much is left?

6   Mr Brown is 46 years old. How old will he be in 28 years' time?

Partitioning, calculating and checking

 Plug in

Answer each question and write more related facts so that you have two additions and two subtractions, like this:

| 5 + 7 = 12 | 7 + 5 = 12 | 12 – 5 = 7 | 12 – 7 = 5 |

a   8 + 3 =

b   16 – 7 =

c   25 – 9 =

 Chat room (1)

Talk to a partner about which method below you prefer to use to answer the question:

$$38 + 46$$

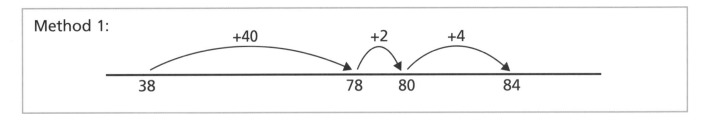

Method 1:

+40   +2   +4

38   78   80   84

Method 2:
$$38 \quad + \quad 46$$
$$30 + 8 \quad + \quad 40 + 6 \quad = 70 + 14 = 84$$

 Power up

Choose any four of these additions and find the answers, using the method you prefer.

28 + 37   53 + 26   47 + 34   26 + 17

55 + 26   45 + 27   18 + 64   37 + 27

Now, for each addition you chose, write related facts so that you have two additions and two subtractions. Check your answers by making sure all four statements are true.

Chat room (2)

Talk to a partner about which method below you prefer to use to answer this question.

$$64 - 19$$

Method 1:

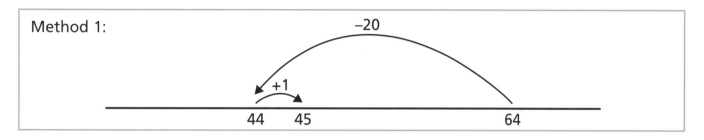

−20

+1

44   45   64

Method 2:

$$64 - 19$$
$$64 - 10 - 9$$
$$54 - 9$$
$$54 - 4 - 5$$
$$50 - 5 = 45$$

 ## Game play

2 Players

You will need: PCM 3, a counter each, a dice and some coloured pencils.

- Read the instructions and play the game to practise adding and subtracting 2-digit numbers.

 Explore

Use the digits shown to make as many different addition and subtraction questions as you can.

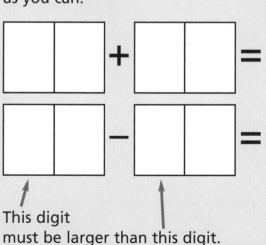

+ =

− =

 9   **2**   **3**   **7**

This digit must be larger than this digit.

Answer each question in your head and check your answers using the inverse operation.

Making decisions about calculations

 Plug in

Write A, B, C or D to show which is the missing number.

a 93 + ☐ = 100   A: 6   B: 8   C: 7   D: 5

b 52 + ☐ = 100   A: 68   B: 58   C: 47   D: 48

c 36 + ☐ = 100   A: 63   B: 74   C: 64   D: 73

d 29 + ☐ = 100   A: 81   B: 71   C: 61   D: 91

e 84 + ☐ = 100   A: 23   B: 24   C: 16   D: 26

 Power up

Which person is suggesting the most sensible number sentence to show each situation?

1 Tariq bought some apples that cost £8. He paid with a £20 note. How much change did he get?

 20 + ☐ = 8   ☐ + 20 = 8    20 − 8 = ☐    8 − 20 = ☐

2 There were 40 avocados in a shop. Sam sold some of them and then had 15 left. How many did he sell?

 ☐ − 15 = 40   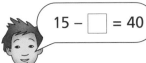 15 − ☐ = 40    ☐ − 40 = 15    40 − ☐ = 15

3 There were some peaches in a shop. Serena sold 14 of them and had 11 left. How many were there at the start?

 14 − ☐ = 11    ☐ − 14 = 11    11 − 14 = ☐    14 − 11 = ☐

 Chat room

Talk to a partner about which of these you could do in your head and which you would need to write something down for. Talk about whether you would use addition or subtraction to solve each of them.

| 35 + 40 = ☐ | ☐ − 58 = 92 | 100 − ☐ = 22 | ☐ + 44 = 100 |

Game play

2 players

You will need: the cards from PCM 4 and counters in two colours.

- Spread the cards face down on the table.
- Take turns to pick a card.
- Read the problem and think about how you would solve it.
- Find a number sentence below that matches it (there may be more than one match).
- Place a counter in your colour on the number sentence.
- The winner is the first player to have five counters on touching sentences.

47 + 85 = __	85 – 47 = __	47 – 38 = __
47 + __ = 100	85 – __ = 47	__ – 38 = 47
__ + 38 = 85	85 + 38 = __	100 – __ = 85
100 + 47 = __	100 – 38 = __	47 + 38 = __
100 – 47 = __	__ – 47 = 85	__ + 85 = 100
47 + __ = 100	100 – 85 = __	__ – 38 = 47

 ## Explore

Copy these shapes or draw your own.
Write the difference between the numbers joined by each rod.

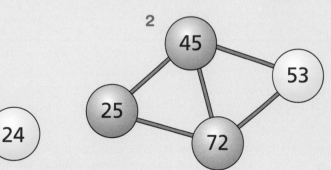

You could draw more of your own shapes like these.

Choosing and using efficient methods

 Plug in

The length of each line below can be found by subtracting the start number from the end number. Write a subtraction question for each and find the length of the line.

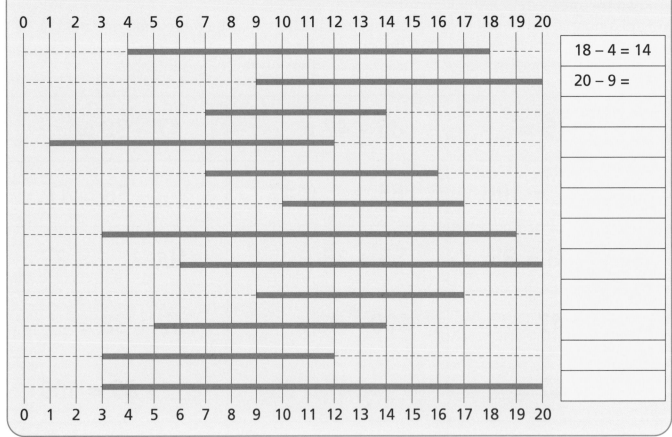

18 − 4 = 14
20 − 9 =

 Chat room

The number lines below have been used to find a difference. Tell a partner about whether you prefer to find a difference by counting up from the smaller number, or by counting back from the larger number.

74 − 27 =

74 − 27 =

 Power up

1 Pick four pairs of numbers, one from each bag. Draw number lines to find their differences, using either of the two methods above.

2 Check each answer to the questions you have made in question 1 by adding the answer to the number chosen from the second bag. Do you get the first number each time?

3 Pick pairs of numbers, one from each bag. Estimate the **total** by rounding the numbers. Then find the total, using a suitable method. Show your working. Compare your methods with others in your group.

 ## Game play

2 players
You will need: four dice.

- Both players roll two dice each and make a 2-digit number.
- Write it down and repeat to make another 2-digit number.
- Now estimate whose total will be the larger. Add the numbers to see.
- The player with the larger total scores a point.
- The winner is the first player to score four points.

= 64

 ## Explore

For each of these weighing problems, write a number sentence to show what you will do. Decide on the best method to find the answer. Be careful, as some of the questions look similar but are not!

1
Sandeep weighs 12 kg more than Lauren.
Lauren weighs 32 kg.
How much does Sandeep weigh?

Sandeep Lauren

2
Jay weighs 17 kg more than Ho-Yan.
Jay weighs 46 kg.
How much does Ho-Yan weigh?

Jay   Ho-Yan

3
Milly weighs 18 kg less than Harry.
Milly weighs 27 kg.
How much does Harry weigh?

Milly   Harry

4
Baz weighs 29 kg less than Hiro.
Hiro weighs 65 kg.
How much does Baz weigh?

Baz   Hiro

Understanding multiplication

 Plug in

1   Count on in 5s from 0 to 50.

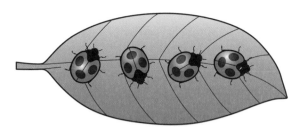

2   Count on in 3s from 0 to 30.

3   Count on in 4s from 0 to 40.

4   Count on in 6s from 0 to 60.

 Power up

The spots on the ladybirds on each leaf can be written as an addition fact or as multiplication facts, like this:

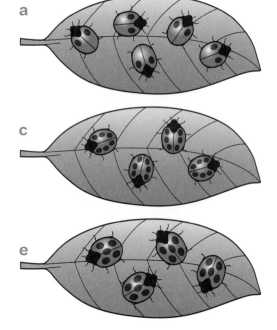

$3 + 3 + 3 + 3 = 12$

$4 \times 3 = 12$ or $3 \times 4 = 12$

1   Write one addition fact and two multiplication facts for the number of spots on the ladybirds on each leaf.

a

b

c

d

e

f

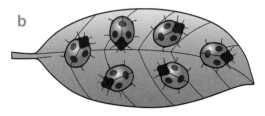
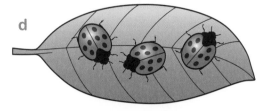
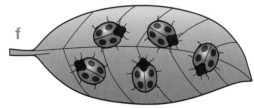

2   What do you notice about the number of spots on the last two leaves?

 # Game play
2 players

You will need: the cards from PCM 5.

- Cut out the cards and play Snap with a partner.
- Call 'Snap' if you make a match between a picture and an addition or multiplication statement.

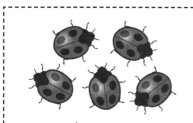 | $4 + 4 + 4 + 4 + 4 = 20$ | $5 \times 4 = 20$

 ## Chat room

There are some ladybirds on the other side of this leaf. The multiplication 5×7 can be used to show the number of spots. Talk to a partner about how many ladybirds there could be and how many spots each might have. Is there more than one possible answer? Why?

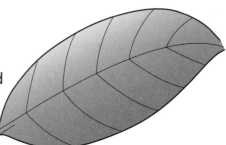

 ## Explore

Write a number sentence for each of these problems using the fact in the red box to help you.

$$6 \times 4 = 24$$

1 There are 4 tins of beans in a pack. How many tins in 6 packs?

2 A school organises some children into 4 teams. Each team has 60 children. How many children are there altogether?

3 A packet of crisps costs 40p. How much does it cost to buy 6 packets?

4 24 children are put into teams of 6. How many teams are there?

5 Hiro used a calculator. He started at zero and kept adding 6. He added 6 forty times in total. What was the final answer he reached?

Understanding division

 Plug in

Count back in equal steps to zero to complete each sequence.

1   Count back in 3s.   30 27 24 ___ ___ ___ ___ ___ ___ ___ 0

2   Count back in 4s.   40 36 32 ___ ___ ___ ___ ___ ___ ___ 0

3   Count back in 6s.   60 54 48 ___ ___ ___ ___ ___ ___ ___ 0

 Chat room

With a partner, look at how Grandad and Grandma organise their pills.

Grandad has 21 pills.
He makes groups of 7.

Grandma also has 21 pills.
She shares out the pills into 7 groups.

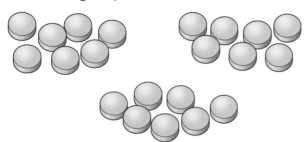

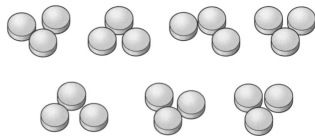

He has 3 groups.

She has 3 pills in each group.

Both ways can be described as 21 ÷ 7 = 3.

Talk about what is different about the ways that Grandad and Grandma organise their pills.

 Power up

You need 24 cubes. Sort the cubes to match one of these division questions. Draw a picture of how you sorted them and write the answer.

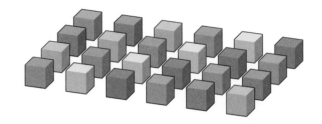

| 24 ÷ 4 = | 24 ÷ 2 = | 24 ÷ 8 = | 24 ÷ 3 = | 24 ÷ 6 = | 24 ÷ 12 = |

Try other divisions from the list in the same way.

Game play

1 player

You will need: the cards from PCM 6.

- Place the cards from PCM 6 below to make as many different true statements as you can.
- Score a point for each different one you can find.

	are shared between	

Each person is given

- Record each statement you make using numbers and a division (÷) sign.

 Explore

Write a number sentence for each of these problems using the fact in the red box to help you.

$$28 \div 4 = 7$$

1   28 children are put into teams of 7. How many teams are there?

2   Mrs Jones has £280. She shares the amount between her 4 children. How much do they each get?

3   Seven people win £280 on the Lottery. They share it equally. How much do they each get?

4   Milly used a calculator. She started with the number 28 and kept taking away 4. How many times did she subtract 4 to reach 0?

5   A coach can carry 40 children. How many coaches are needed to transport 280 children?

6   Amina spends £4 on bus fare every day. How much does she spend in 7 days?

Using multiplication strategies

 Plug in

How quickly can you answer these times-tables questions?

a 5 × 4   b 4 × 2   c 3 × 3   d 7 × 2   e 4 × 4   f 5 × 3   g 6 × 2

h 1 × 8   i 4 × 6   j 5 × 0   k 10 × 7   l 5 × 5   m 5 × 9   n 4 × 3

 Power up (1)

The bumps on these building bricks form an **array**.

Write two multiplication facts for each brick.

$2 \times 4 = 8$

$4 \times 2 = 8$

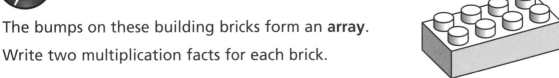

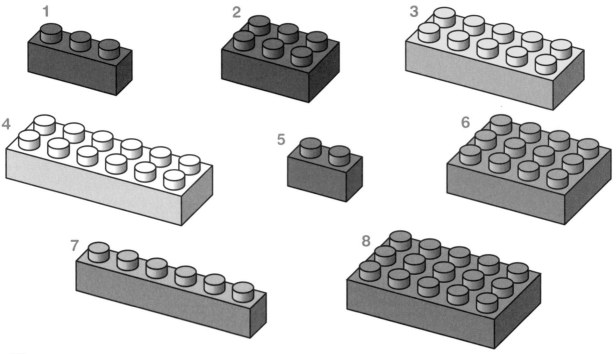

 Game play

1 player

You will need: squared paper and a dice.

- Roll the dice and multiply the two numbers together. Record the multiplication fact, e.g. 6 × 4 = 24.

- Draw a rectangle onto squared paper to show the multiplication fact as an array and count the squares to check your answer.

Chat room

Arrays can be used to help you multiply numbers. Talk to a partner about how these arrays are split to make multiplying simpler. See if you can work out 3 × 15 using the second diagram.

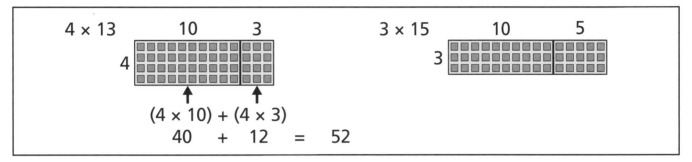

4 × 13   10   3   3 × 15   10   5

(4 × 10) + (4 × 3)
40   +   12   =   52

 Power up (2)

Match each of the questions to a diagram and use it to help you answer the question.

5 × 17 =

3 × 18 =

4 × 23 =

3 × 26 =

7 × 15 =

a
	10	8
3	3 × 10	3 × 8

b
	20	3
4	4 × 20	4 × 3

c
	20	6
3	3 × 20	3 × 6

d
	10	5
7	7 × 10	7 × 5

e
	10	7
5	5 × 10	5 × 7

 Explore

Use a similar approach to help you solve these problems.

1   Joe bought 4 bars of chocolate, each costing 27p. How much did he pay?

2   Each bag of sweets holds 28 sweets. How many sweets in 3 bags?

3   Li ran for 35 minutes every day for a week. How many minutes did she run for?

Using division strategies

 Plug in

Each triangle tile has three numbers. They can be used to write some multiplication and division facts. Write four facts using the numbers.

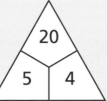

$20 \div 5 = 4$
$20 \div 4 = 5$
$5 \times 4 = 20$
$4 \times 5 = 20$

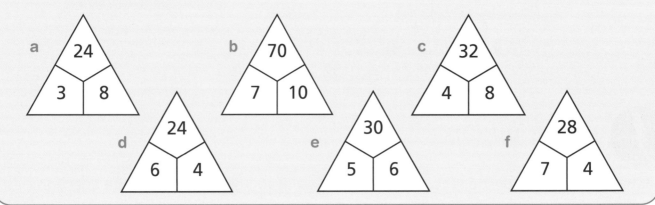

a 24 — 3, 8

b 70 — 7, 10

c 32 — 4, 8

d 24 — 6, 4

e 30 — 5, 6

f 28 — 7, 4

 Chat room

Talk to a partner about the method of division shown below.

$72 \div 4$	72	
	40	10×4
	32	
	20	5×4
	12	
	12	3×4
	0	

Answer = 10 + 5 + 3 = 18

$88 \div 3$	88	
	60	20×3
	28	
	15	5×3
	13	
	12	4×3
	1	

Answer = 20 + 5 + 4 = 29 r1

 Power up

Use the method above to solve these questions.

a $93 \div 5$ b $69 \div 3$ c $87 \div 4$
d $96 \div 4$ e $82 \div 3$ f $98 \div 3$

For each question that you have answered, write two related multiplication facts and one division fact.

Game play

2 players

You will need 3 dice.

- Take turns to roll the 3 dice to make a 2-digit number divided by a single-digit number, as shown for these dice.
- Both players work out the answer.
- If the answer has a remainder, this is your score.
- If the answer does not have a remainder, you score five points.
- The winner is the first player to score 20 points.

64 ÷ 3

64 ÷ 3 = 21 r1

Explore

Pam works at a post office and customers are always asking her questions. Work with a partner to help Pam solve each problem.

How many 5p stamps can I buy with 72p?

I need 59 envelopes. How many packs of 4 must I buy?

How many 3p stamps can I buy with 88p?

I need 34 envelopes. How many packs of 4 must I buy?

I need 93 envelopes. How many packs of 4 must I buy?

How many 5p stamps can I buy with 83p?

How many 4p stamps can I buy with 79p?

I need 77 pencils. How many packs of 10 must I buy?

How many 3p stamps can I buy with 98p?

I need 66 envelopes. How many packs of 4 must I buy?

How many 6p stamps can I buy with 86p?

I need 84 pencils. How many packs of 10 must I buy?

Finding fractions

 Plug in

Use the answers to your 3 times-table to help you answer these questions.

a $\frac{1}{3}$ of 12   b $\frac{1}{3}$ of 9   c $\frac{1}{3}$ of 15   d $\frac{1}{3}$ of 27   e $\frac{1}{3}$ of 30

f $\frac{1}{3}$ of 6   g $\frac{1}{3}$ of 21   h $\frac{1}{3}$ of 18   i $\frac{1}{3}$ of 3   j $\frac{1}{3}$ of 24

 Power up (1)

Each bag below holds some money.

A   B   C   D   E

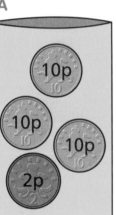

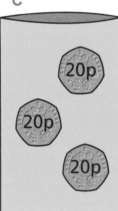

Work out these fractions of the amounts of money.

a $\frac{1}{2}$ of **A**   b $\frac{1}{5}$ of **B**   c $\frac{1}{6}$ of **C**   d $\frac{1}{3}$ of **D**   e $\frac{1}{12}$ of **E**

f $\frac{1}{4}$ of **A**   g $\frac{1}{9}$ of **B**   h $\frac{1}{5}$ of **C**   i $\frac{1}{9}$ of **D**   j $\frac{1}{6}$ of **E**

 Chat room

Do you agree or disagree with each statement?

1 If $\frac{1}{4}$ of some money is 5p, then $\frac{3}{4}$ must be 15p.

2 If $\frac{1}{3}$ of some money is 10p, then $\frac{2}{3}$ must be 20p.

3 If $\frac{1}{9}$ of some money is 8p, then $\frac{5}{9}$ must be 30p.

4 If $\frac{1}{7}$ of some money is 12p, then $\frac{2}{7}$ must be 24p.

5 If $\frac{1}{8}$ of some money is 3p, then $\frac{7}{8}$ must be 18p.

Now explain to a partner what you have learnt about finding fractions of numbers.

Power up (2)

Find these fractions of the bags of money opposite.

a $\frac{3}{4}$ of **A**   b $\frac{4}{5}$ of **B**   c $\frac{5}{6}$ of **C**   d $\frac{2}{3}$ of **D**   e $\frac{7}{12}$ of **E**

f $\frac{3}{8}$ of **A**   g $\frac{4}{9}$ of **B**   h $\frac{3}{5}$ of **C**   i $\frac{2}{9}$ of **D**   j $\frac{5}{6}$ of **E**

 ## Game play

2+ players

You will need: cards from the top of PCM 7.

- Spread all the cards face down.
- Each player picks a card and finds how many gold coins he/she will be given.
- The player with the highest number wins a point.
- The winner is the first player to score 8 points.

 ## Explore

There were 120 sailors on the Goodship Lollipop. Use division to find the number of sailors:

$\frac{1}{4}$ **were seasick: 120 ÷ 4 = 30 sailors**

a $\frac{1}{6}$ of sailors had wooden legs.

b $\frac{1}{12}$ of sailors were homesick.

c $\frac{3}{10}$ of sailors owned a parrot.

d $\frac{5}{6}$ of sailors hated the biscuits onboard.

e $\frac{1}{60}$ of sailors had eye patches.

f $\frac{3}{20}$ of sailors fell overboard.

g $\frac{5}{12}$ of sailors owned a cat.

h $\frac{4}{5}$ of sailors had scars.

i $\frac{7}{30}$ of sailors had walked the plank.

Comparing and describing 2-D shapes

Plug in

Write the missing words or shapes in these sequences.

1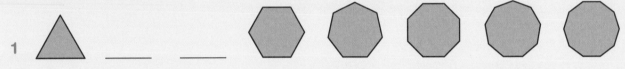

2 triangle, quadrilateral, ____ , ____ , heptagon, ____ , nonagon, decagon

Chat room

Talk to a partner about what is similar about the shapes in each pair and what is different.

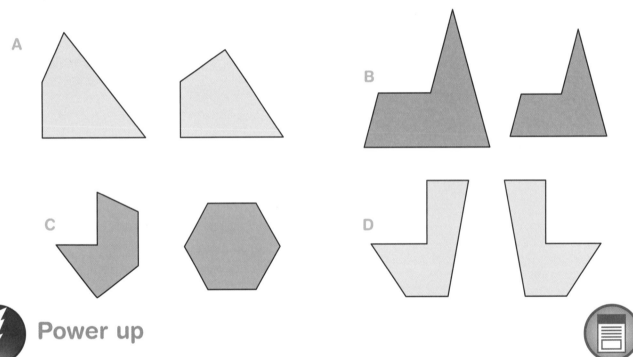

Power up

Draw the first Venn diagram shown below onto a large sheet of paper.
Use cards from PCM 8. Work with a friend to place each shape into the correct region of your Venn diagram. Repeat for the second diagram.

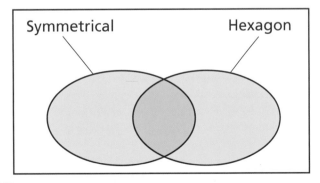

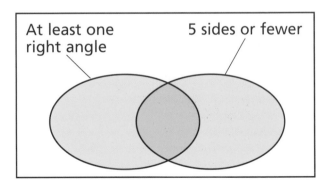

 # Game play

2 players

You will need: a counter each.

- Each player chooses one of these rules:
  - Jump only on shapes that have more than 5 sides.
  - Jump only on shapes which have at least 1 right angle.
  - Jump only on symmetrical shapes.
  - Jump only on quadrilaterals.
- Place your counter at the bottom side of the square below.
- Take turns to make a move according to your rule. You can move one place each time (vertically, horizontally or diagonally).
- The first player to reach the top side is the winner.

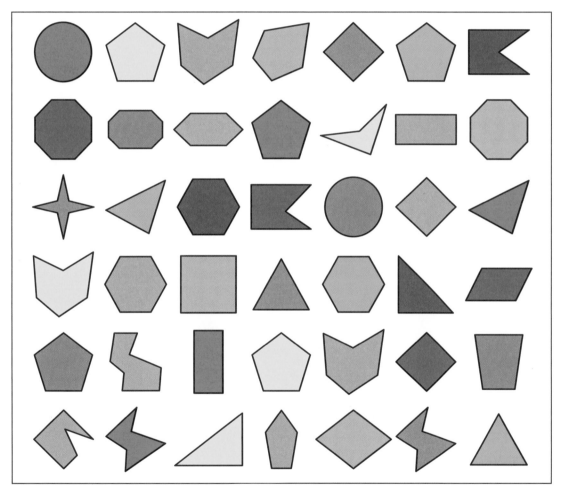

Start somewhere along this side.

 ## Explore

Draw a shape to match each description.

1 It has 3 sides and 1 right angle.   2 It has 4 equal sides and 4 right angles.

3 It has 5 sides and is symmetrical.   4 It has 4 sides but none of them are equal.

Compare your shapes with a friend. Are they the same or different?

Comparing and describing 3-D shapes

 Plug in

Write the missing words or numbers.

1   A cube has _____ faces, 8 vertices and 12 edges.

2   A cone has 1 flat and 1 curved face. It has _____ vertex and _____ edge.

3   A sphere has no _____ or _____ and just 1 curved face.

4   A cylinder has _____ edges and _____ faces. It has no vertices.

Chat room

Talk to partner about what is similar about the shapes in each pair and what is different.

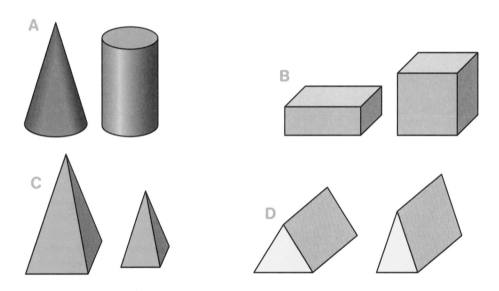

Power up

Draw the first Venn diagram shown below onto a large sheet of paper. Using solid shapes, work with a friend to place each into the correct region of your Venn diagram. Repeat for the second diagram.

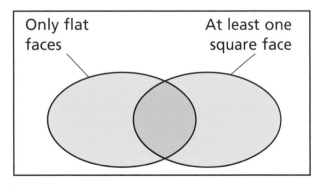

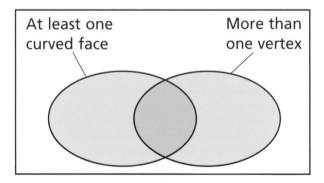

 **Game play**

2 players

You will need: counters in two colours and a dice.

- Roll the dice and read the related clue. Place a counter in your colour on a shape that matches the clue.

- The winner is the player with counters on the most shapes at the end of the game.

All its faces are squares.

It is symmetrical.

It has a triangular face.

It has no flat faces.

It has a circular face.

It has only rectangular faces.

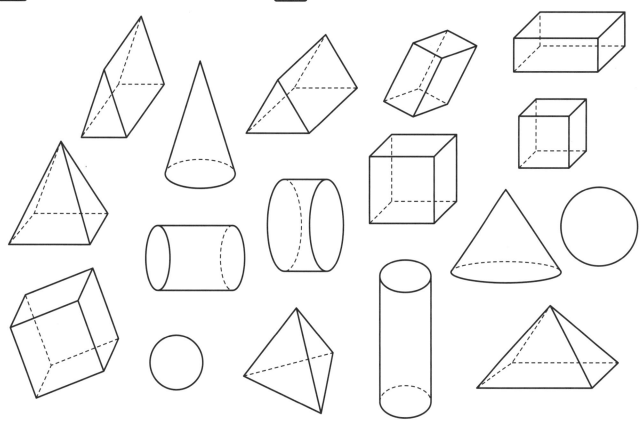

 Explore

Match each object to its description.

A It is small and has 2 circular faces. It is a cylinder.

B It is a cuboid with all rectangular faces and 8 vertices.

C It is a type of prism with 2 triangular faces.

Make up some more clues of your own for other objects.

Sorting and using appropriate shape vocabulary

 Plug in

Write **true** or **false** for each of these statements.
1 A cuboid has 1 curved face.
2 A cylinder has 2 edges and 3 faces.
3 A shape with 6 sides is called an octagon.
4 A regular triangle is an equilateral triangle.
5 If a shape has all sides equal and all angles equal, we say it is regular.

 Game play

2 players

You will need: a counter each and a dice.

- Roll the dice and draw and name the shape you land on.

- If you do it correctly, stay where you are. If not, move back 4 spaces. The winner is the first to reach the finish.

START	a shape with five sides	a shape with four straight sides	a shape with three sides and one right angle	a shape with three right angles
	a shape that has one curved side	a shape with ten straight sides	a shape that is regular	a shape that is half a circle
	a shape with four lines of symmetry		a shape that is not regular	a symmetrical shape
		FINISH		
	a shape with four sides but none are equal	a scalene triangle	an equilateral triangle	a shape with no right angles
	a regular quadrilateral	a shape with one right angle	a symmetrical shape with six sides	a shape with two right angles and four sides
	a shape with six straight sides	a shape with more than four sides	a semicircle	a shape with five straight sides
	a shape that is not symmetrical	a shape with eight straight sides	a shape with two lines of symmetry	a shape with one line of symmetry

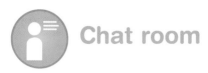 **Chat room**

Each present is a different shape. Talk to a partner about the names of the shapes.

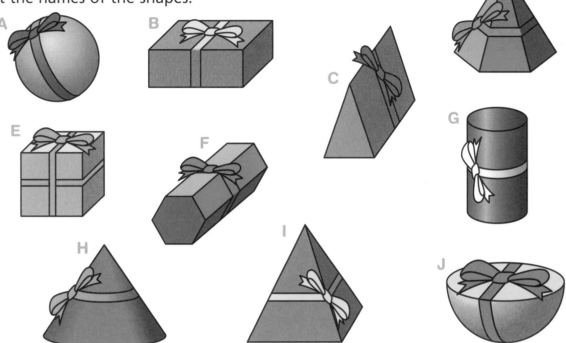

 Power up

Copy this Carroll diagram onto a large sheet of paper.

With a partner, work out where each present would go in the diagram.

	At least one circular face	No circular faces
A prism		
Not a prism		

 Explore

Can you work out which present each of these children brought?

1 Caz's present has 6 rectangular faces and 2 hexagonal ones.

2 Sam's present has 1 circular face and 1 vertex.

3 Joe's present has 6 triangular faces and a hexagonal one.

4 Dev's present has 1 circular face, 1 flat face, 1 curved edge and no vertices.

5 Ben's present has 2 circular faces, 2 curved edges and no vertices.

6 Li's present has 6 square faces, 12 vertices and 8 edges.

Generating and extending patterns

Plug in

Which shape is next in each rotation sequence? Choose from the box and write the letter each time.

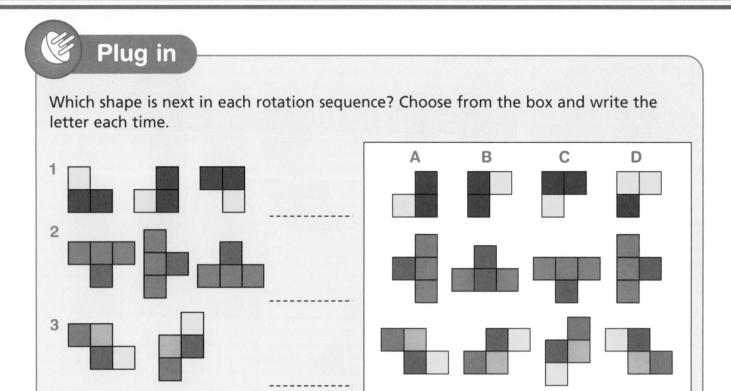

1 _____

2 _____

3 _____

Power up

Your teacher will give you some dotted paper.

1 Draw boxes around sets of 4 × 4 dots. In each box, draw a different hexagon.

2 Tick any of the hexagons you have drawn that are symmetrical.

3 Write how many right angles each hexagon has next to the shape.

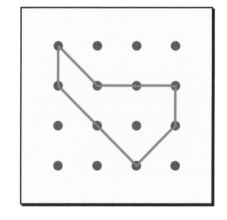

Chat room

1 Talk to a partner about these shapes. Work out how many cubes there are in each.

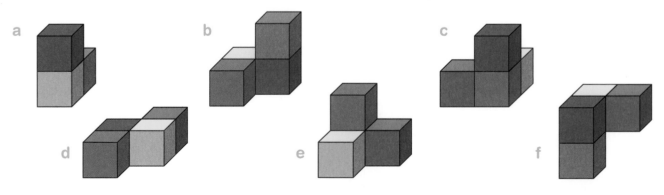

a   b   c   d   e   f

2 Can you make the shapes using your own cubes? Are any of the shapes the same?

Game play

2 players

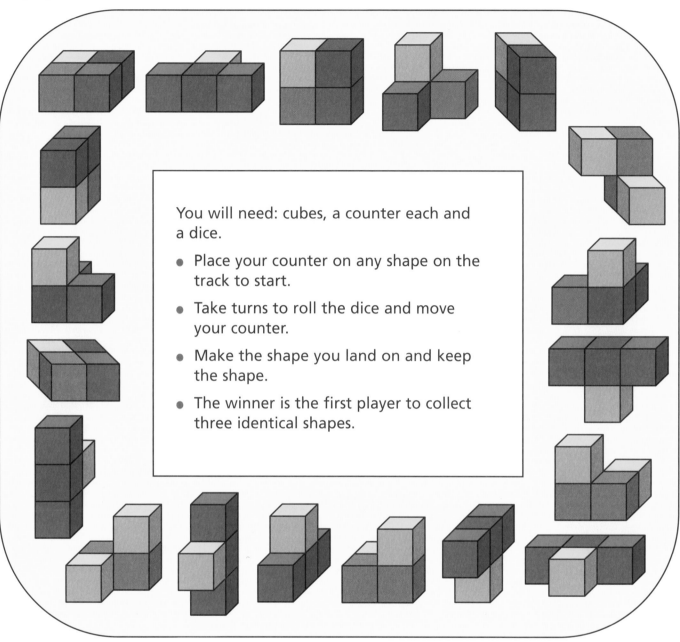

You will need: cubes, a counter each and a dice.

- Place your counter on any shape on the track to start.

- Take turns to roll the dice and move your counter.

- Make the shape you land on and keep the shape.

- The winner is the first player to collect three identical shapes.

 Explore

Your teacher will give you some dotted paper. Can you draw:

1 a regular quadrilateral?

2 a pentagon with 3 right angles?

3 a triangle with 2 equal sides (an isosceles triangle)?

Compare your answers with other pupils in your class. Are your shapes the same or different?

Interpreting and solving word problems

 Plug in

Answer these questions as quickly as you can.

a $6 + 12 + 5$	b $3 \times 5 - 10$	c $10 + 24 - 8$	d $7 \times 2 \times 2$
e $90 \div 10 \times 2$	f $35 \div 5 + 8$	g $5 + 8 + 9$	h $4 \times 4 \div 8$

 Power up (1)

It costs £5 per adult and £3 per child to go ice skating.

£5 per adult
£3 per child

1   How much does it cost for:

a   2 adults?

b   4 children?

c   4 adults and 2 children?

d   1 adult and 3 children?

e   3 adults and 3 children?

f   5 adults and 4 children?

2   How much change would you get from £20 if you bought tickets for:

a   2 adults?

b   5 children?

c   1 adult and 3 children?

3   How many adults can go for the same price as 10 children?

4   How many children can go for the same price as 12 adults?

 Chat room

Talk to a partner about how you solved the parts in question 2. Can you write number sentences to show what you did?

Power up (2)

It costs £2 per person to hire skates at the same ice rink.

£5 per adult
£3 per child
and £2 skate hire

1 How much does it cost, including skate hire for:

a 2 adults?

b 3 children?

c 2 adults and 2 children?

d 1 adult and 3 children?

e 3 adults and 3 children?

f 5 adults and 4 children?

2 Can you write a number sentence to show how you worked out each part?

 ## Game play

2+ players

You will need: loop cards from PCM 9.

- Share the cards out between the group. Read out the start question and answer it.
- The person with the answer on their card reads the next question out, and so on.
- Put all the cards in order – now look at the letters – what do you notice?

 ### Explore

£5 per adult
£3 per child
and £2 skate hire

A group of adults and children have £30 to spend on ice skating. All of them need to hire skates.

Here are some different ways the money could be used.

- 4 adults could go with £2 change.
- 2 adults and 3 children could go with £1 change.

Find as many other ways the money could be used as you can.

Checking answers and using units of measure

Plug in

Write the missing numbers.

a 1 metre = _____ centimetres

b 1 kilogram = _____ grams

c 1 litre = _____ millilitres

d 1 kilometre = _____ metres

e 4 kilograms = _____ grams

f 3 metres = _____ centimetres

g 6 litres = _____ millilitres

h 8 kilometres = _____ metres

i $\frac{1}{2}$ metre = _____ centimetres

j $\frac{1}{2}$ kilogram = _____ grams

k $\frac{1}{4}$ kilogram = _____ grams

l $\frac{1}{4}$ kilometre = _____ metres

Chat room

Talk to a partner about the meaning of this statement.

Do you agree with the statement? Why?

> For every problem, decide what to do, then estimate, calculate and check the answer is sensible.

Power up (1)

For each problem follow the advice of the statement above to find the answer. Work with a partner.

1 The total mass of these three parcels is 1 kg.
   What is the mass of the third parcel?

500 g   250 g   ?

2 The total mass of these three parcels is 2 kg.
   What is the mass of the largest parcel?

?   350 g   350 g

3 Four identical parcels each weigh 125 g.
   What is the total mass of the parcels?

125 g 125 g 125 g 125 g

4 The total mass of these parcels is 2 kg.
   Two have the same mass and the smaller one weighs 200 g.
   What is the mass of one of the larger ones?

?   ?   200 g

5   Two identical parcels together weigh 900 g.
    A smaller parcel weighs 100 g less than one of them.
    What is its mass?

6   The larger parcel is 3 times heavier than the smaller one.
    The smaller one weighs 200 g.
    What is the total mass of the parcels?

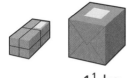

$1\frac{1}{2}$ kg

7   The larger parcel is 3 times heavier than the smaller one.
    The larger one weighs $1\frac{1}{2}$ kg.
    What is the total mass of the parcels?

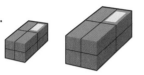

8   Two identical parcels each weigh $\frac{1}{2}$ kg.
    A larger parcel weighs 250 g more than one of them.
    What is the total mass of the parcels?

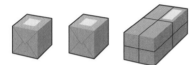

 ## Game play

2+ players

You will need: loop cards from PCM 10.

- Share the cards out between the group. Read out the start question and answer it.

- The person with the answer on their card reads the next question out, and so on.

- Put all the cards in order – now look at the letters – what do you notice?

 ## Explore

Use these athletics facts to help you write some problems
of your own for a friend to solve.

	Long jump	Weight lifting	100 m sprint time
Jenny Jumper	4 m	9 kg	15 seconds
Harry Stretch	250 cm	9100 g	$\frac{1}{4}$ minute
Sarah Strider	2 m 80 cm	8 kg 600 g	$16\frac{1}{2}$ seconds
Ivor Step	$3\frac{1}{2}$ m	$8\frac{3}{4}$ kg	16.5 seconds

Ask questions that include words such as *How much further … ?*
How much more … ? How much altogether … ?
How many centimetres less … ? How much faster … ?

Do you notice anything about the 100 m sprint times?
Talk to a partner about what you notice.

Using time lines to find time differences

Plug in

Continue these time sequences.

a   8:00 8:30 9:00 9:30 ___ ___ ___ ___ ___ ___ ___ 1:30

b   3:15 3:30 3:45 4:00 ___ ___ ___ ___ ___ ___ ___ 6:00

c   5:00 5:05 5:10 ___ ___ ___ ___ ___ ___ ___ ___ 5:55

d   2:30 2:35 2:40 ___ ___ ___ ___ ___ ___ ___ ___ 3:25

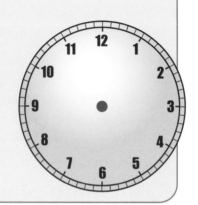

Chat room (1)

Tell a partner how you could use the lines below to work out how long it is between 3:30 and 6:15.

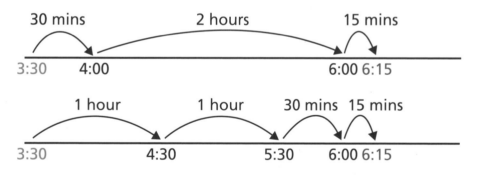

Which line do you find easier? Why?

Power up (1)

Solve these problems using number lines like the ones above to help you. How long is each of these films?

1	2	3
MONSTERS AT WORK!	**Mouse in the House!**	**The Planet Vrog!**
Starts at 8:15	**Starts at 6:45**	**Starts at 7:30**
Finishes at 10:00	**Finishes at 8:30**	**Finishes at 9:45**

Chat room (2)

Tell a partner how you could use the lines below to work out what time a film started if it lasted for $3\frac{3}{4}$ hours and finished at 9:30.

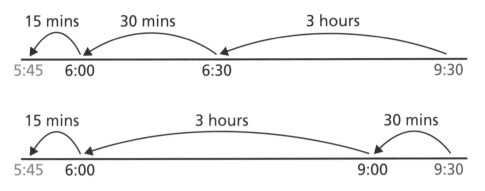

Which line do you find easier? Why?

 ## Power up (2)

Use number lines like the ones above, to help you work out what time each film started.

1

SKYSCRAPERS!
Lasts $2\frac{1}{2}$ hours
Finishes at 9:15

2

Ice Attack!
Lasts $1\frac{3}{4}$ hours
Finishes at 9:15

3

Poodle Power!
Lasts $1\frac{3}{4}$ hours
Finishes at 8:45

 ## Game play

2 players

You will need: PCM 11, a counter and a dice.

● Read the instructions and play the game with a friend.

 ## Explore

Look at your school timetable.

Work out what time each lesson would start if your school day started at 6:30 in the morning.

What time would your school day end?

Plug in

Count on or back in 5s to continue these sequences. Write 10 numbers in each sequence.

a 5 10 15 20 ____   b 100 95 90 ____   c 75 80 85 ____

 Chat room

Talk about the information below with a partner.

A frequency table shows us how many times something happens or how many things we have. To record data we can use **tallying**, where we group data in fives, like this: 卌. We then write the frequency (or total) alongside. We can show the information on a bar graph or a pictogram.

Frequency table showing how many birds visited a bird table in 1 hour

Type	Tally	Frequency
Blackbird	卌	5
Robin	II	2
Sparrow	卌 II	7
Magpie	IIII	4
Greenfinch	卌 IIII	9

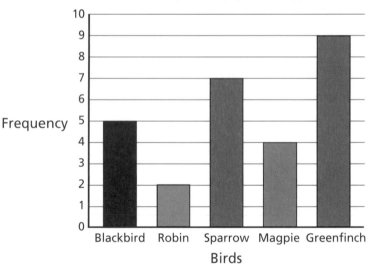

Birds at bird table in 1 hour

Pictogram showing how many of each type of bird visited the bird table in 1 hour

Blackbird	🐦🐦🐦
Robin	🐦
Sparrow	🐦🐦🐦
Magpie	🐦
Greenfinch	🐦🐦🐦🐦

🐦 = 2 birds

> Do all the charts show the same information?

Power up

Each child in Class C has coloured a picture to show what colour eyes they have.

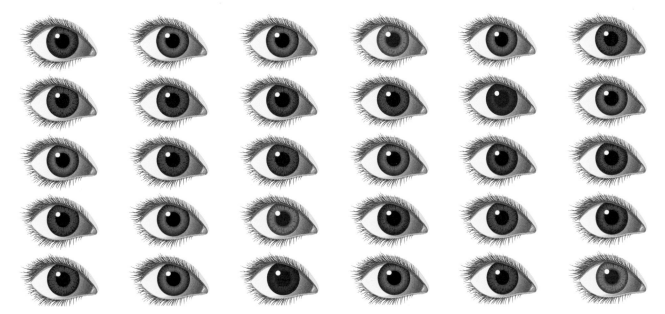

1   Draw a frequency table to show the number of children with each eye colour: green, blue, brown, black and grey.

2   Now draw a bar chart or a pictogram to show the information.
    Remember to label your chart clearly and to write a key for your pictogram.

 ## Game play

2 players

You will need: PCM 12.

● With a partner, follow the trail and fill in the missing answers.

● How quickly can you work them out?

 ## Explore

Carry out your own survey of the colour of eyes of pupils in your class.

Alternatively, you could find out some other information, such as:

● how many teeth each pupil in your class has

● how many people live in their house

● the number of pets they have

OR

● how many times they can write their name in a minute.

Draw a pictogram or bar chart of the information you found.

Interpreting data in tables and graphs

 Plug in

How quickly can you write the answers to these questions?

a 6 + 7	b 17 − 9	c 9 + 7	d 7 + 8	e 12 − 5	f 14 + 7	g 4 + 8
h 14 − 8	i 13 + 8	j 15 − 8	k 17 + 5	l 14 − 9	m 16 − 7	n 16 + 5

 Chat room

Talk to a partner about what you think each of these tables and graphs is showing.

Table showing how many yellow cards players in these teams were given over a three-month period

	Jan	Feb	Mar
Manchester United	8	15	21
Chelsea	16	11	7
Arsenal	9	10	12

Bar chart showing the number of cubes children can hold in one hand

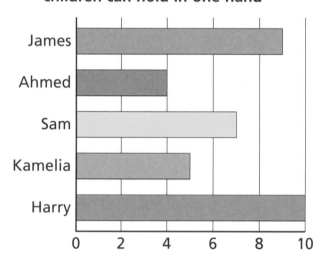

Average heights of dinosaurs

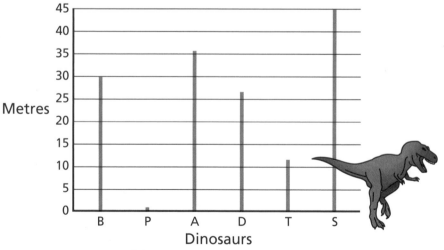

B = Brachiosaurus   P = Pisanosaurus
A = Argentinasaurus   D = Diplodocus
T = Tyrannosaurus   S = Seismosaurus

Venn digram showing whole numbers to 20

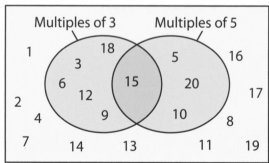

Power up

1 Answer these questions about the charts and tables on page 58.

  a   How many cubes can Sam hold in one hand?

  b   How many more cubes can Harry hold than Ahmed?

  c   How many cubes can all 5 children hold in total?

  d   How many yellow cards did Chelsea get in February?

  e   How many yellow cards did Arsenal get in March?

  f   Approximately what was the average height of a tyrannosaurus?

  g   About how much taller was a seismosaurus than a brachiosaurus?

  h   How many numbers to 20 are multiples of 3?

  i   How many of the numbers to 20 are multiples of both 3 and 5?

2 Copy this Carroll diagram. Sort the numbers from 1 to 20 into it. Then compare it with the Venn diagram on page 58.

	Multiples of 3	Not multiples of 3
Multiples of 5		
Not multiples of 5		

 Game play

2 players

This table shows the number of times the numbers 1 to 6 were rolled by two people when they each rolled a dice 100 times.

	1	2	3	4	5	6
Player 1	15	21	17	18	14	15
Player 2	16	13	16	20	19	16

You will need: a dice each.

- Decide who is player 1 and who is player 2.

- Both players roll a dice and find their corresponding number in the table.

- The higher number scores a point. The winner is the first to reach 8 points.

 Explore

Look on the Internet or in newspapers or magazine for charts, tables and graphs.

Can you work out what each is showing?

Understanding scales and intervals

 Plug in

Count on in:

a   10s from 0 to 100.

b   10s from 200 to 300.

c   5s from 120 to 170.

d   2s from 300 to 320.

e   20s from 200 to 400.

f   25s from 0 to 250.

 Game play

2 players
You will need: PCM 13, a dice and a blue coloured pencil each.

• Play the game with a partner.

 Chat room

Work with a partner.
Discuss and work out
what number each arrow
is pointing to.

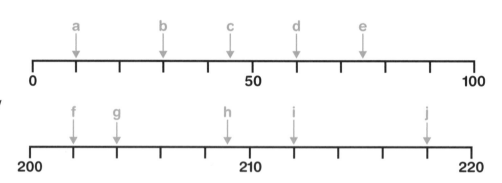

 Power up

This bar-line graph shows the height of a male African elephant at different ages in his life.

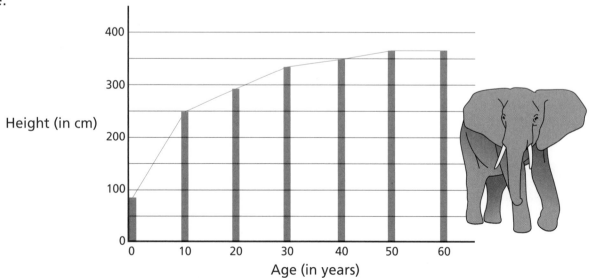

Look at the bar-line graph on page 60 to find out the answers to these questions.

1   About how tall is a male elephant aged:

   a 20?   b 40?   c 10?   d 5?   e 50?   f 30?

2   This chart shows the height of a female African elephant.

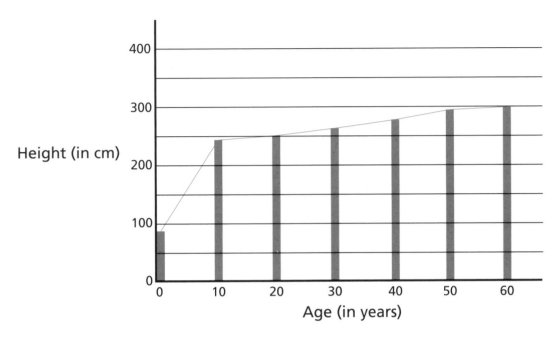

About how tall is a female elephant aged:

   a 20?   b 40?   c 10?   d 5?   e 50?   f 30?

 Explore

This chart can help you to convert from inches to centimetres or from centimetres to inches. Use the chart to work out some approximate relationships, for example 50 cm is about 20 inches.

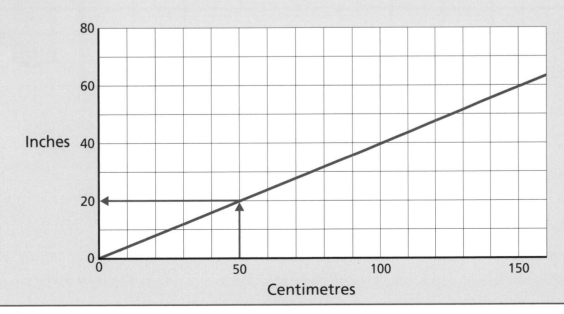

Choosing and carrying out calculations

Plug in

1 What value lies exactly halfway between the two numbers on each scale below?

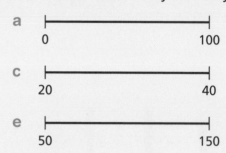

a
0   100

b
100   200

c
20   40

d
0   500

e
50   150

f
500   1000

2 What value lies exactly a quarter of the way between the two numbers on each scale above?

Chat room

Talk to a partner about this bar-line graph and what you think it shows.

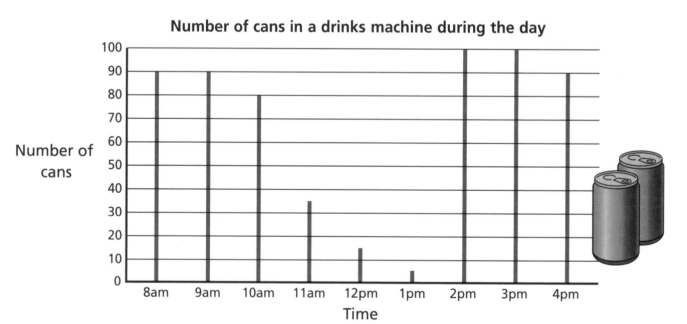

Number of cans in a drinks machine during the day

Number of cans

Time

Power up

1 How many cans of drink were sold between:

a 8am and 9am?
d 11am and 12pm?

b 9am and 10am?
e 12pm and 1pm?

c 10am and 11am?
f 3pm and 4pm?

2   Between which two hours were the most cans sold?

3   a   What do you think happened between 1pm and 2pm?
     b   Where might this drinks machine be?
     c   Why do you think no cans were sold between 2pm and 3pm?
     d   If no cans were sold between 1pm and 2pm, how many cans were sold in total
          between 8am and 4pm?

 Game play

2+ players

- Each person in your group should write three question cards about the information
  shown in the bar-line graph below.
- Make sure you write the correct answer too!
- Use questions such as *How many snacks were in the machine at ... ?*
  How many were sold between ... ? How many more ... ? How many altogether ... ?

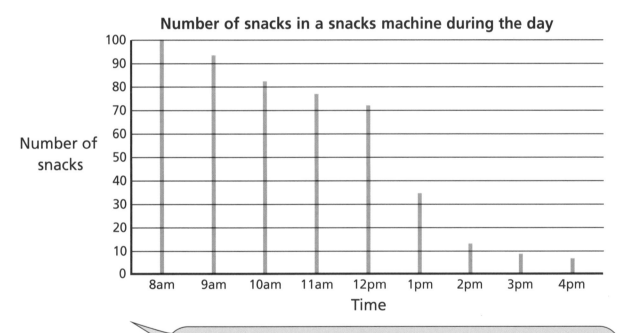

Number of snacks in a snacks machine during the day

Give the cards to your teacher to read out as a group quiz.

 Explore

The table shows the total number of drinks and snacks sold during one school week.

1   How many drinks and snacks
     were sold on Tuesday?

2   How many snacks were sold
     during this school week?

3   How many drinks were sold
     during this school week?

	Mon	Tue	Wed	Thu	Fri
Drinks	78	94	67	88	100
Snacks	89	80	56	92	99

Write some more questions of your own to answer.